W9-BNT-824

DOVER · THRIFT · EDITIONS

The Mikado

WILLIAM SCHWENCK GILBERT

Illustrated by the Author

DOVER PUBLICATIONS, INC.
New York

DOVER THRIFT EDITIONS

GENERAL EDITOR: STANLEY APPELBAUM
EDITOR OF THIS VOLUME: PHILIP SMITH

Theatrical Rights

This Dover Thrift Edition may be used in its entirety, in adaptation or in any other way for theatrical productions, professional and amateur, in the United States, without fee, permission or acknowledgment. (This may not apply outside of the United States, as copyright conditions may vary.)

Copyright © 1992 by Dover Publications, Inc.
All rights reserved under Pan American and International Copyright Conventions.

Published in Canada by General Publishing Company, Ltd., 30 Lesmill Road, Don Mills, Toronto, Ontario.
Published in the United Kingdom by Constable and Company, Ltd., 3 The Lanchesters, 162–164 Fulham Palace Road, London W6 9ER.

This Dover edition, first published in 1992, contains the standard performance text of *The Mikado* (first produced in 1885). The author's illustrations are taken from *The Bab Ballads*, Second Edition, George Routledge and Sons, Limited, London and New York, 1898. A new introductory Note has been specially prepared for this edition.

Manufactured in the United States of America
Dover Publications, Inc., 31 East 2nd Street, Mineola, N.Y. 11501

Library of Congress Cataloging-in-Publication Data

Sullivan, Arthur, Sir, 1842–1900.
    [Mikado. Libretto]
    The Mikado / William Schwenck Gilbert : illustrated by the author.
        p.   cm. — (Dover thrift editions)
    "Contains the standard performance text of The Mikado (first produced in 1885). The author's illustrations are taken from The Bab ballads, second edition, George Routledge and Sons, Limited, London and New York, 1898. A new introductory note has been specially prepared for this edition"—T.p. verso.
    ISBN 0-486-27268-0 (pbk.)
    1. Operas—Librettos.   I. Gilbert, W. S. (William Schwenck), 1836–1911.   II. Title.   III. Series.
ML50.S96M4   1992
782.1'2'0268—dc20   92–24015
                                                                        CIP
                                                                        MN

Note

ALTHOUGH the British playwright and humorist William Schwenck Gilbert (1836–1911) is today chiefly remembered through productions of his comic operas with music by Arthur Sullivan (1842–1900), he was in his day highly regarded as an author of humorous verse and prose and as a skilled comic artist. His libretto for *The Mikado, or, The Town of Titipu* (1885), the most popular of the Gilbert and Sullivan collaborations, reveals his wit at its pinnacle, transforming a light farce (with only the thinnest of Japanese elements) into a perennially amusing satire of Victorian England, and of human society and behavior in general.

Gilbert's drawings, taken from a popular collection of his verse, reinforce the text's comic value, and represent an additional side of his creativity.

Contents

Dramatis Personæ

THE MIKADO OF JAPAN

NANKI-POO (*his Son, disguised as a wandering minstrel, and in love with* YUM-YUM)

KO-KO (*Lord High Executioner of Titipu*)

POOH-BAH (*Lord High Everything Else*)

PISH-TUSH (*a Noble Lord*)

YUM-YUM
PITTI-SING } *Three Sisters—Wards of* KO-KO
PEEP-BO

KATISHA (*an elderly Lady, in love with* NANKI-POO)

Chorus of School-girls, Nobles, Guards, and Coolies

ACT I

COURTYARD OF KO-KO'S OFFICIAL RESIDENCE.

ACT II

KO-KO'S GARDEN.

First produced at the Savoy Theatre on March 14, 1885

Act I

SCENE.—*Courtyard of* KO-KO's *Palace in Titipu. Japanese nobles discovered standing and sitting in attitudes suggested by native drawings.*

CHORUS OF NOBLES

If you want to know who we are,
    We are gentlemen of Japan;
On many a vase and jar—
    On many a screen and fan,
        We figure in lively paint:
        Our attitude's queer and quaint—
        You're wrong if you think it ain't, oh!

If you think we are worked by strings,
    Like a Japanese marionette,
You don't understand these things:
    It is simply Court etiquette.
        Perhaps you suppose this throng
        Can't keep it up all day long?
        If that's your idea, you're wrong, oh!

Enter NANKI-POO *in great excitement. He carries a native guitar on his back and a bundle of ballads in his hand.*

RECIT.—NANKI-POO

Gentlemen, I pray you tell me
Where a gentle maiden dwelleth,
Named Yum-Yum, the ward of Ko-Ko?
In pity speak—oh, speak, I pray you!

1

A NOBLE. Why, who are you who ask this question?

NANK. Come gather round me, and I'll tell you.

SONG AND CHORUS—NANKI-POO

A wandering minstrel I—
 A thing of shreds and patches,
 Of ballads, songs and snatches,
And dreamy lullaby!

My catalogue is long,
 Through every passion ranging,
 And to your humours changing
I tune my supple song!

  Are you in sentimental mood?
   I'll sigh with you,
    Oh, sorrow, sorrow!
  On maiden's coldness do you brood?
   I'll do so, too—
    Oh, sorrow, sorrow!
  I'll charm your willing ears
  With songs of lovers' fears,
  While sympathetic tears
   My cheeks bedew—
    Oh, sorrow, sorrow!

But if patriotic sentiment is wanted,
 I've patriotic ballads cut and dried;
For where'er our country's banner may be planted,
 All other local banners are defied!
Our warriors, in serried ranks assembled,
 Never quail—or they conceal it if they do—
And I shouldn't be surprised if nations trembled
 Before the mighty troops of Titipu!

CHORUS. We shouldn't be surprised, etc.

NANK. And if you call for a song of the sea,
  We'll heave the capstan round,
  With a yeo heave ho, for the wind is free,

Her anchor's a-trip and her helm's a-lee,
Hurrah for the homeward bound!

CHORUS.   Yeo-ho—heave ho—
Hurrah for the homeward bound!

To lay aloft in a howling breeze
May tickle a landsman's taste,
But the happiest hour a sailor sees
Is when he's down
At an inland town,
With his Nancy on his knees, yeo ho!
And his arm around her waist!

CHORUS.   Then man the capstan—off we go,
As the fiddler swings us round,
With a yeo heave ho,
And a rumbelow,
Hurrah for the homeward bound!

A wandering minstrel I, etc.

Enter PISH-TUSH

PISH. And what may be your business with Yum-Yum?

NANK. I'll tell you. A year ago I was a member of the Titipu town band. It was my duty to take the cap round for contributions. While discharging this delicate office, I saw Yum-Yum. We loved each other at once, but she was betrothed to her guardian Ko-Ko, a cheap tailor, and I saw that my suit was hopeless. Overwhelmed with despair, I quitted the town. Judge of my delight when I heard, a month ago, that Ko-Ko had been condemned to death for flirting! I hurried back at once, in the hope of finding Yum-Yum at liberty to listen to my protestations.

PISH. It is true that Ko-Ko was condemned to death for flirting, but he was reprieved at the last moment, and raised to the exalted rank of Lord High Executioner under the following remarkable circumstances:

SONG—PISH-TUSH *and* CHORUS

Our great Mikado, virtuous man,

When he to rule our land began,
> Resolved to try
> A plan whereby
> Young men might best be steadied.
So he decreed, in words succinct,
That all who flirted, leered or winked
(Unless connubially linked),
> Should forthwith be beheaded.

>> And I expect you'll all agree
>> That he was right to so decree.
>>> And I am right,
>>> And you are right,
>> And all is right as right can be!

CHORUS.
>> And you are right,
>> And we are right, etc.

This stern decree, you'll understand,
Caused great dismay throughout the land!
> For young and old
> And shy and bold
> Were equally affected.
The youth who winked a roving eye,
Or breathed a non-connubial sigh,
Was thereupon condemned to die—
> He usually objected.

>> And you'll allow, as I expect,
>> That he was right to so object.
>>> And I am right,
>>> And you are right,
>> And everything is quite correct!

CHORUS.
>> And you are right,
>> And we are right, etc.

And so we straight let out on bail,
A convict from the county jail,
> Whose head was next

On some pretext
Condemnëd to be mown off,
And made *him* Headsman, for we said,
"Who's next to be decapited
Cannot cut off another's head
Until he's cut his own off."

And we are right, I think you'll say,
To argue in this kind of way;
And I am right,
And you are right,
And all is right—too-looral-lay!

CHORUS.   And you are right,
                 And we are right, etc.

[*Exeunt* CHORUS.

Enter POOH-BAH

NANK. Ko-Ko, the cheap tailor, Lord High Executioner of Titipu! Why, that's the highest rank a citizen can attain!

POOH. It is. Our logical Mikado, seeing no moral difference between the dignified judge who condemns a criminal to die, and the industrious mechanic who carries out the sentence, has rolled the two offices into one, and every judge is now his own executioner.

NANK. But how good of you (for I see that you are a nobleman of the highest rank) to condescend to tell all this to me, a mere strolling minstrel!

POOH. Don't mention it. I am, in point of fact, a particularly haughty and exclusive person, of pre-Adamite ancestral descent. You will understand this when I tell you that I can trace my ancestry back to a protoplasmal primordial atomic globule. Consequently, my family pride is something inconceivable. I can't help it. I was born sneering. But I struggle hard to overcome this defect. I mortify my pride continually. When all the great officers of State resigned in a body, because they were too proud to serve under an ex-tailor, did I not unhesitatingly accept all their posts at once?

PISH. And the salaries attached to them? You did.

POOH. It is consequently my degrading duty to serve this upstart as

First Lord of the Treasury, Lord Chief Justice, Commander-in-Chief, Lord High Admiral, Master of the Buckhounds, Groom of the Back Stairs, Archbishop of Titipu, and Lord Mayor, both acting and elect, all rolled into one. And at a salary! A Pooh-Bah paid for his services! I a salaried minion! But I do it! It revolts me, but I do it!

NANK. And it does you credit.

POOH. But I don't stop at that. I go and dine with middle-class people on reasonable terms. I dance at cheap suburban parties for a moderate fee. I accept refreshment at any hands, however lowly. I also retail State secrets at a very low figure. For instance, any further information about Yum-Yum would come under the head of a State secret. (NANKI-POO *takes the hint, and gives him money.*) (*Aside.*) Another insult, and, I think, a light one!

SONG—POOH-BAH *with* NANKI-POO *and* PISH-TUSH

> Young man, despair,
> 　　Likewise go to,
> Yum-Yum the fair
> 　　You must not woo.
> 　　It will not do:
> 　　I'm sorry for you,
> You very imperfect ablutioner!
> 　　This very day
> 　　From school Yum-Yum
> Will wend her way,
> 　　And homeward come,
> 　　With beat of drum
> 　　And a rum-tum-tum,
> To wed the Lord High Executioner!
> 　　And the brass will crash,
> 　　And the trumpets bray,
> And they'll cut a dash
> 　　On their wedding day.
> She'll toddle away, as all aver,
> With the Lord High Executioner!

NANK. *and* POOH.　　　And the brass will crash, etc.

It's a hopeless case,
        As you may see,
And in your place
        Away I'd flee;
        But don't blame me—
        I'm sorry to be
Of your pleasure a diminutioner.
        They'll vow their pact
        Extremely soon,
In point of fact
        This afternoon.
        Her honeymoon
        With that buffoon
At seven commences, so *you* shun her!

ALL.   And the brass will crash, etc.

                                        [*Exit* PISH-TUSH.

RECIT.—NANKI-POO *and* POOH-BAH

NANK.   And I have journeyed for a month, or nearly,
         To learn that Yum-Yum, whom I love so dearly,
         This day to Ko-Ko is to be united!
POOH.   The fact appears to be as you've recited:
         But here he comes, equipped as suits his station;
         He'll give you any further information.

                    [*Exeunt* POOH-BAH *and* NANKI-POO.

                Enter CHORUS OF NOBLES

Behold the Lord High Executioner
    A personage of noble rank and title—
A dignified and potent officer,
    Whose functions are particularly vital!
        Defer, defer,
    To the Lord High Executioner!

            Enter KO-KO *attended*

SOLO—KO-KO

Taken from the county jail
   By a set of curious chances;
Liberated then on bail,
   On my own recognizances;
Wafted by a favouring gale
   As one sometimes is in trances,
To a height that few can scale,
   Save by long and weary dances;
Surely, never had a male
   Under such like circumstances
So adventurous a tale
   Which may rank with most romances.

CHORUS.   Defer, defer,
    To the Lord High Executioner, etc.

KO. Gentlemen, I'm much troubled by this reception. I can only trust that by strict attention to duty I shall ensure a continuance of those favours which it will ever be my study to deserve. If I should ever be called upon to act professionally, I am happy to think that there will be no difficulty in finding plenty of people whose loss will be a distinct gain to society at large.

SONG—KO-KO *with* CHORUS OF MEN

As some day it may happen that a victim must be found,

I've got a little list—I've got a little list
Of society offenders who might well be underground,
   And who never would be missed—who never would be missed!
There's the pestilential nuisances who write for autographs—
All people who have flabby hands and irritating laughs—
All children who are up in dates, and floor you with 'em flat—
All persons who in shaking hands, shake hands with you like *that*—
And all third persons who on spoiling *tête-à-têtes* insist—
   They'd none of 'em be missed—they'd none of 'em be missed!

CHORUS. He's got 'em on the list—he's got 'em on the list;
            And they'll none of 'em be missed—they'll none of 'em be
            missed.

There's the banjo serenader[1], and the others of his race,
   And the piano-organist—I've got him on the list!
And the people who eat peppermint and puff it in your face,
   They never would be missed—they never would be missed!
Then the idiot who praises, with enthusiastic tone,
All centuries but this, and every country but his own;
And the lady from the provinces, who dresses like a guy,
And who "doesn't think she waltzes, but would rather like to try";
And that singular anomaly, the lady novelist—
   I don't think she'd be missed—I'm *sure* she'd not be missed!

CHORUS. He's got her on the list—he's got her on the list;
            And I don't think she'll be missed—I'm *sure* she'll not be
            missed!

And that *Nisi Prius* nuisance, who just now is rather rife,
   The Judicial humorist—I've got *him* on the list!
All funny fellows, comic men, and clowns of private life—
   They'd none of 'em be missed—they'd none of 'em be missed.
And apologetic statesmen of a compromising kind,
Such as—What d'ye call him—Thing'em-bob, and likewise—Never-
      mind,
And 'St—'st—'st—and What's-his-name, and also You-know-who—
The task of filling up the blanks I'd rather leave to *you*.

---

[1] This phrase originally read "nigger serenader," in reference to blackface entertainers of England during the Victorian minstrel craze. The alternative wording was adopted in the 1940s to prevent offense.

But it really doesn't matter whom you put upon the list,
   For they'd none of 'em be missed—they'd none of 'em be missed!

CHORUS. You may put 'em on the list—you may put 'em on the list;
          And they'll none of 'em be missed—they'll none of 'em be
          missed!

Enter POOH-BAH

KO. Pooh-Bah, it seems that the festivities in connection with my approaching marriage must last a week. I should like to do it handsomely, and I want to consult you as to the amount I ought to spend upon them.

POOH. Certainly. In which of my capacities? As First Lord of the Treasury, Lord Chamberlain, Attorney-General, Chancellor of the Exchequer, Privy Purse, or Private Secretary?

KO. Suppose we say as Private Secretary.

POOH. Speaking as your Private Secretary, I should say that, as the city will have to pay for it, don't stint yourself, do it well.

KO. Exactly—as the city will have to pay for it. That is your advice.

POOH. As Private Secretary. Of course you will understand that, as Chancellor of the Exchequer, I am bound to see that due economy is observed.

KO. Oh! But you said just now "Don't stint yourself, do it well."

POOH. As Private Secretary.

KO. And now you say that due economy must be observed.

POOH. As Chancellor of the Exchequer.

KO. I see. Come over here, where the Chancellor can't hear us. (*They cross the stage.*) Now, as my Solicitor, how do you advise me to deal with this difficulty?

POOH. Oh, as your Solicitor, I should have no hesitation in saying "Chance it——"

KO. Thank you. (*Shaking his hand.*) I will.

POOH. If it were not that, as Lord Chief Justice, I am bound to see that the law isn't violated.

KO. I see. Come over here where the Chief Justice can't hear us. (*They cross the stage.*) Now, then, as First Lord of the Treasury?

POOH. Of course, as First Lord of the Treasury, I could propose a special vote that would cover all expenses, if it were not that, as Leader of the Opposition, it would be my duty to resist it, tooth and nail. Or, as Paymaster-General, I could so cook the accounts that, as Lord High Auditor, I should never discover the fraud. But then, as Archbishop of Titipu, it would be my duty to denounce my dishonesty and give myself into my own custody as First Commissioner of Police.

KO. That's extremely awkward.

POOH. I don't say that all these distinguished people couldn't be squared; but it is right to tell you that they wouldn't be sufficiently degraded in their own estimation unless they were insulted with a very considerable bribe.

KO. The matter shall have my careful consideration. But my bride and her sisters approach, and any little compliment on your part, such as an abject grovel in a characteristic Japanese attitude, would be esteemed a favour.

[*Exeunt together.*

Enter procession of YUM-YUM's *schoolfellows, heralding*
YUM-YUM, PEEP-BO, *and* PITTI-SING

CHORUS OF GIRLS

Comes a train of little ladies
    From scholastic trammels free,
Each a little bit afraid is,
    Wondering what the world can be!

Is it but a world of trouble—
    Sadness set to song?
Is its beauty but a bubble
    Bound to break ere long?

Are its palaces and pleasures
    Fantasies that fade?
And the glory of its treasures
    Shadow of a shade?

Schoolgirls we, eighteen and under,
    From scholastic trammels free,
And we wonder—how we wonder!—
    What on earth the world can be!

TRIO

YUM-YUM, PEEP-BO, *and* PITTI-SING, *with* CHORUS OF GIRLS

THE THREE.   Three little maids from school are we,
                Pert as a school-girl well can be,
                Filled to the brim with girlish glee,
                    Three little maids from school!
YUM-YUM.   Everything is a source of fun. (*Chuckle.*)
PEEP-BO.   Nobody's safe, for we care for none! (*Chuckle.*)
PITTI-SING.   Life is a joke that's just begun! (*Chuckle.*)
THE THREE.   Three little maids from school!
ALL (*dancing*). Three little maids who, all unwary,
                Come from a ladies' seminary,
                Freed from its genius tutelary—
THE THREE (*suddenly demure*). Three little maids from school!

YUM-YUM.   One little maid is a bride, Yum-Yum—

PEEP-BO.   Two little maids in attendance come—
PITTI-SING.   Three little maids is the total sum.
THE THREE.   Three little maids from school!
YUM-YUM.   From three little maids take one away.
PEEP-BO.   Two little maids remain, and they—
PITTI-SING.   Won't have to wait very long, they say—
THE THREE.   Three little maids from school!
ALL (*dancing*). Three little maids who, all unwary,
                 Come from a ladies' seminary,
                 Freed from its genius tutelary—
THE THREE (*suddenly demure*). Three little maids from school!

Enter KO-KO *and* POOH-BAH

KO. At last, my bride that is to be! (*About to embrace her.*)

YUM. You're not going to kiss me before all these people?

KO. Well, that was the idea.

YUM. (*aside to* PEEP-BO). It seems odd, doesn't it?

PEEP. It's rather peculiar.

PITTI. Oh, I expect it's all right. Must have a beginning, you know.

YUM. Well, of course I know nothing about these things; but I've no objection if it's usual.

KO. Oh, it's quite usual, I think. Eh, Lord Chamberlain? (*Appealing to* POOH-BAH.)

POOH. I have known it done. (KO-KO *embraces her.*)

YUM. Thank goodness that's over! (*Sees* NANKI-POO, *and rushes to him.*) Why, that's never you? (*The Three Girls rush to him and shake his hands, all speaking at once.*)

YUM. Oh, I'm so glad! I haven't seen you for ever so long, and I'm right at the top of the school, and I've got three prizes, and I've come home for good, and I'm not going back any more!

PEEP. And have you got an engagement?—Yum-Yum's got one, but she doesn't like it, and she'd ever so much rather it was you! I've come home for good, and I'm not going back any more!

PITTI. Now tell us all the news, because you go about everywhere, and we've been at school, but, thank goodness, that's all over now, and we've come home for good, and we're not going back any more!

(*These three speeches are spoken together in one breath.*)

KO. I beg your pardon. Will you present me?

YUM. ⎧ Oh, this is the musician who used——
PEEP. ⎨ Oh, this is the gentleman who used——
PITTI. ⎩ Oh, it is only Nanki-Poo who used——

KO. One at a time, if you please.

YUM. Oh, if you please, he's the gentleman who used to play so beautifully on the—on the——

PITTI. On the ~~Marine Parade~~. *Esplanade*

YUM. Yes, I think that was the name of the instrument.

NANK. Sir, I have the misfortune to love your ward, Yum-Yum—oh, I know I deserve your anger!

KO. Anger! not a bit, my boy. Why, I love her myself. Charming little girl, isn't she? Pretty eyes, nice hair. Taking little thing, altogether. Very glad to hear my opinion backed by a competent authority. Thank you very much. Good-bye. (*To* PISH-TUSH.) Take him away. (PISH-TUSH *removes him.*)

PITTI. (*who has been examining* POOH-BAH). I beg your pardon, but what is this? Customer come to try on?

KO. That is a Tremendous Swell.

PITTI. Oh, it's alive. (*She starts back in alarm.*)

POOH. Go away, little girls. Can't talk to little girls like you. Go away, there's dears.

KO. Allow me to present you, Pooh-Bah. These are my three wards. The one in the middle is my bride elect.

POOH. What do you want me to do to them? Mind, I *will not* kiss them.

KO. No, no, you shan't kiss them; a little bow—a mere nothing—you needn't mean it, you know.

POOH. It goes against the grain. They are not young ladies, they are young persons.

KO. Come, come, make an effort, there's a good nobleman.

POOH. (*aside to* KO-KO). Well, I shan't mean it. (*With a great effort.*) How de do, little girls, how de do? (*Aside.*) Oh, my protoplasmal ancestor!

KO. That's very good. (*Girls indulge in suppressed laughter.*)

POOH. I see nothing to laugh at. It is very painful to me to have to say "How de do, little girls, how de do?" to young persons. I'm not in the habit of saying "How de do, little girls, how de do?" to anybody under the rank of a Stockbroker.

KO. (*aside to girls*). Don't laugh at him, he can't help it—he's under treatment for it. (*Aside to* POOH-BAH.) Never mind them, they don't understand the delicacy of your position.

POOH. We know how delicate it is, don't we?

KO. I should think we did! How a nobleman of your importance can do it at all is a thing I never can, never shall understand.

[KO-KO *retires up and goes off.*

QUARTET AND CHORUS OF GIRLS
YUM-YUM, PEEP-BO, PITTI-SING, *and* POOH-BAH

YUM., PEEP. *and* PITTI.	So please you, Sir, we much regret If we have failed in etiquette Towards a man of rank so high— We shall know better by and by.

YUM.	But youth, of course, must have its fling,
	   So pardon us,
	   So pardon us,

PITTI.	And don't, in girlhood's happy spring,
	   Be hard on us,
	   Be hard on us,
	If we're inclined to dance and sing.
	   Tra la la, etc. (*Dancing.*)

CHORUS OF GIRLS.   But youth, of course, must have its fling, etc.

POOH.	I think you ought to recollect
	You cannot show too much respect
	Towards the highly titled few;
	But nobody does, and why should you?
	That youth at us should have its fling,
	   Is hard on us,
	   Is hard on us;
	To our prerogative we cling—
	   So pardon us,
	   So pardon us,
	If we decline to dance and sing.
	   Tra la la, etc. (*Dancing.*)

CHORUS OF GIRLS.   But youth, of course, must have its fling, etc.

[*Exeunt all but* YUM-YUM.

Enter NANKI-POO

NANK. Yum-Yum, at last we are alone! I have sought you night and day for three weeks, in the belief that your guardian was beheaded, and I find that you are about to be married to him this afternoon!

YUM. Alas, yes!

NANK. But you do not love him?

YUM. Alas, no!

NANK. Modified rapture! But why do you not refuse him?

YUM. What good would that do? He's my guardian, and he wouldn't let me marry you!

NANK. But I would wait until you were of age!

YUM. You forget that in Japan girls do not arrive at years of discretion until they are fifty.

NANK. True; from seventeen to forty-nine are considered years of indiscretion.

YUM. Besides—a wandering minstrel, who plays a wind instrument outside tea-houses, is hardly a fitting husband for the ward of a Lord High Executioner.

NANK. But—— (*Aside.*) Shall I tell her? Yes! She will not betray me! (*Aloud.*) What if it should prove that, after all, I am no musician?

YUM. There! I was certain of it, directly I heard you play!

NANK. What if it should prove that I am no other than the son of his Majesty the Mikado?

YUM. The son of the Mikado! But why is your Highness disguised? And what has your Highness done? And will your Highness promise never to do it again?

NANK. Some years ago I had the misfortune to captivate Katisha, an elderly lady of my father's Court. She misconstrued my customary affability into expressions of affection, and claimed me in marriage, under my father's law. My father, the Lucius Junius Brutus of his race, ordered me to marry her within a week, or perish ignominiously on the scaffold. That night I fled his Court, and, assuming the disguise of a Second Trombone, I joined the band in which you found me when I had the happiness of seeing you! (*Approaching her.*)

YUM (*retreating*). If you please, I think your Highness had better not come too near. The laws against flirting are excessively severe.

NANK. But we are quite alone, and nobody can see us.

YUM. Still, that don't make it right. To flirt is capital.

NANK. It *is* capital!

YUM. And we must obey the law.

NANK. Deuce take the law!

YUM. I wish it would, but it won't!

NANK. If it were not for that, how happy we might be!

YUM. Happy indeed!

NANK. If it were not for the law, we should now be sitting side by side, like that. (*Sits by her.*)

YUM. Instead of being obliged to sit half a mile off, like that. (*Crosses and sits at other side of stage.*)

NANK. We should be gazing into each other's eyes, like that. (*Gazing at her sentimentally.*)

YUM. Breathing sighs of unutterable love—like that. (*Sighing and gazing lovingly at him.*)

NANK. With our arms round each other's waists, like that. (*Embracing her.*)

YUM. Yes, if it wasn't for the law.

NANK. If it wasn't for the law.

YUM. As it is, of course we couldn't do anything of the kind.

NANK. Not for worlds!

YUM. Being engaged to Ko-Ko, you know!

NANK. Being engaged to Ko-Ko!

DUET—YUM-YUM *and* NANKI-POO

NANK.
Were you not to Ko-Ko plighted,
   I would say in tender tone,
"Loved one, let us be united—
   Let us be each other's own!"
I would merge all rank and station,
   Worldly sneers are nought to us,
And, to mark my admiration,
   I would kiss you fondly thus—   (*Kisses her.*)

BOTH. $\left. \begin{matrix} I \\ He \end{matrix} \right\}$ would kiss $\left\{ \begin{matrix} you \\ me \end{matrix} \right\}$ fondly thus—(*Kiss.*)

YUM.	But as I'm engaged to Ko-Ko, To embrace you thus, *con fuoco*, Would distinctly be no *giuoco*, And for yam I should get toko—

BOTH.	Toko, toko, toko, toko!

NANK.	So, in spite of all temptation,
	   Such a theme I'll not discuss,
	And on no consideration
	   Will I kiss you fondly thus— (*Kissing her.*)
	
	Let me make it clear to you,
	This is what I'll never do!
	   This, oh, this, oh, this, oh, this— (*Kissing her.*)

TOGETHER.	This, oh, this, etc.

[*Exeunt in opposite directions.*

Enter KO-KO

KO. (*looking after* YUM-YUM). There she goes! To think how entirely my future happiness is wrapped up in that little parcel! Really, it hardly seems worth while! Oh, matrimony!—— (*Enter* POOH-BAH *and* PISH-TUSH.) Now then, what is it? Can't you see I'm soliloquizing? You have interrupted an apostrophe, sir!

PISH. I am the bearer of a letter from his Majesty the Mikado.

KO. (*taking it from him reverentially*). A letter from the Mikado! What in the world can he have to say to me? (*Reads letter.*) Ah, here it is at last! I thought it would come sooner or later! The Mikado is struck by the fact that no executions have taken place in Titipu for a year and decrees that unless somebody is beheaded within one month the post of Lord High Executioner shall be abolished, and the city reduced to the rank of a village!

PISH. But that will involve us all in irretrievable ruin!

KO. Yes. There is no help for it, I shall have to execute somebody at once. The only question is, who shall it be?

POOH. Well, it seems unkind to say so, but as you're already under sentence of death for flirting, everything seems to point to *you*.

KO. To me? What are you talking about? I can't execute myself.

POOH. Why not?

KO. Why not? Because, in the first place, self-decapitation is an extremely difficult, not to say dangerous, thing to attempt; and, in the second, it's suicide, and suicide is a capital offence.

POOH. That is so, no doubt.

PISH. We might reserve that point.

POOH. True, it could be argued six months hence, before the full Court.

KO. Besides, I don't see how a man *can* cut off his own head.

POOH. A man might try.

PISH. Even if you only succeeded in cutting it half off, that would be something.

POOH. It would be taken as an earnest of your desire to comply with the Imperial will.

KO. No. Pardon me, but there I am adamant. As official Headsman, my reputation is at stake, and I can't consent to embark on a professional operation unless I see my way to a successful result.

POOH. This professional conscientiousness is highly creditable to *you*, but it places us in a very awkward position.

KO. My good sir, the awkwardness of your position is grace itself compared with that of a man engaged in the act of cutting off his own head.

PISH. I am afraid that, unless you can obtain a substitute——

KO. A substitute? Oh, certainly—nothing easier. (*To* POOH-BAH.) I appoint you Lord High Substitute.

POOH. I should be delighted. Such an appointment would realize my fondest dreams. But no, at any sacrifice, I must set bounds to my insatiable ambition!

TRIO

KO-KO	POOH-BAH	PISH-TUSH
My brain it teems	I am so proud,	I heard one day
With endless schemes	If I allowed	A gentleman say
Both good and new	My family pride	That criminals who
For Titipu;	To be my guide,	Are cut in two

KO-KO	POOH-BAH	PISH-TUSH
But if I flit,	I'd volunteer	Can hardly feel
The benefit	To quit this sphere	The fatal steel,
That I'd diffuse	Instead of you,	And so are slain
The town would lose!	In a minute or two.	Without much pain.
Now every man	But family pride	If this is true,
To aid his clan	Must be denied,	It's jolly for you;
Should plot and plan	And set aside,	Your courage screw
As best he can,	And mortified.	To bid us adieu,
And so,	And so,	And go
Although	Although	And show
I'm ready to go,	I wish to go,	Both friend and foe
Yet recollect	And greatly pine	How much you dare.
'Twere disrespect	To brightly shine,	I'm quite aware
Did I neglect	And take the line	It's your affair,
To thus effect	Of a hero fine,	Yet I declare
This aim direct,	With grief condign	I'd take your share,
So I object—	I must decline—	But I don't much care—
So I object—	I must decline—	I don't much care—
So I object—	I must decline—	I don't much care—

ALL. To sit in solemn silence in a dull, dark dock,
In a pestilential prison, with a life-long lock,
Awaiting the sensation of a short, sharp shock,
From a cheap and chippy chopper on a big black block!

[*Exeunt* POOH. *and* PISH.

KO. This is simply appalling! I, who allowed myself to be respited at the last moment, simply in order to benefit my native town, am now required to die within a month, and that by a man whom I have loaded with honours! Is this public gratitude? Is this—— (*Enter* NANKI-POO, *with a rope in his hands*.) Go away, sir! How dare you? Am I never to be permitted to soliloquize?

NANK. Oh, go on—don't mind me.

KO. What are you going to do with that rope?

NANK. I am about to terminate an unendurable existence.

KO. Terminate your existence? Oh, nonsense! What for?

NANK. Because you are going to marry the girl I adore.

KO. Nonsense, sir. I won't permit it. I am a humane man, and if you attempt anything of the kind I shall order your instant arrest. Come, sir, desist at once or I summon my guard.

NANK. That's absurd. If you attempt to raise an alarm, I instantly perform the Happy Despatch with this dagger.

KO. No, no, don't do that. This is horrible! (*Suddenly.*) Why, you cold-blooded scoundrel, are you aware that, in taking your life, you are committing a crime which—which—which is—— Oh! (*Struck by an idea.*) Substitute!

NANK. What's the matter?

KO. Is it *absolutely certain* that you are resolved to die?

NANK. Absolutely!

KO. Will *nothing* shake your resolution?

NANK. Nothing.

KO. Threats, entreaties, prayers—all useless?

NANK. All! My mind is made up.

KO. Then, if you really mean what you say, and if you are absolutely resolved to die, and if nothing whatever will shake your determination—don't spoil yourself by committing suicide, but be beheaded handsomely at the hands of the Public Executioner!

NANK. I don't see how that would benefit me.

KO. You don't? Observe: you'll have a month to live, and you'll live like a fighting-cock at my expense. When the day comes there'll be a grand public ceremonial—you'll be the central figure—no one will attempt to deprive you of that distinction. There'll be a procession—bands—dead march—bells tolling—all the girls in tears—Yum-Yum distracted—then, when it's all over, general rejoicings, and a display of fireworks in the evening. *You* won't see them, but they'll be there all the same.

NANK. Do you think Yum-Yum would really be distracted at my death?

KO. I am convinced of it. Bless you, she's the most tender-hearted little creature alive.

NANK. I should be sorry to cause her pain. Perhaps, after all, if I were to withdraw from Japan, and travel in Europe for a couple of years, I might contrive to forget her.

KO. Oh, I don't think you could forget Yum-Yum so easily; and, after all, what is more miserable than a love-blighted life?

NANK. True.

KO. Life without Yum-Yum—why, it seems absurd!

NANK. And yet there are a good many people in the world who have to endure it.

KO. Poor devils, yes! You are quite right not to be of their number.

NANK. (*suddenly*). I *won't* be of their number!

KO. Noble fellow!

NANK. I'll tell you how we'll manage it. Let me marry Yum-Yum to-morrow, and in a month you may behead me.

KO. No, no. I draw the line at Yum-Yum.

NANK. Very good. If you can draw the line, so can I. (*Preparing rope.*)

KO. Stop, stop—listen one moment—be reasonable. How can I consent to your marrying Yum-Yum if I'm going to marry her myself?

NANK. My good friend, she'll be a widow in a month, and you can marry her then.

KO. That's true, of course. I quite see that. But, dear me! my position during the next month will be most unpleasant—most unpleasant.

NANK. Not half so unpleasant as my position at the end of it.

KO. But—dear me!—well—I agree—after all, it's only putting off my wedding for a month. But you won't prejudice her against me, will you? You see, I've educated her to be my wife; she's been taught to regard me as a wise and good man. Now I shouldn't like her views on that point disturbed.

NANK. Trust me, she shall never learn the truth from me.

FINALE

Enter CHORUS, POOH-BAH, *and* PISH-TUSH

CHORUS

With aspect stern
　And gloomy stride,
We come to learn
　How you decide.

Don't hesitate
　Your choice to name,
A dreadful fate
　You'll suffer all the same.

POOH. 　To ask you what you mean to do we punctually appear.

KO. 　Congratulate me, gentlemen, I've found a Volunteer!

ALL.   The Japanese equivalent for Hear, Hear, Hear!
KO. (*presenting him*). 'Tis Nanki-Poo!
ALL.   Hail, Nanki-Poo!
KO.   I think he'll do?
ALL.   Yes, yes, he'll do!
KO.   He yields his life if I'll Yum-Yum surrender.
           Now I adore that girl with passion tender,
           And could not yield her with a ready will,
                        Or her allot
                        If I did not
           Adore myself with passion tenderer still!

           Enter YUM-YUM, PEEP-BO, *and* PITTI-SING

ALL.   Ah, yes!
           He loves himself with passion tenderer still!
KO. (*to* NANKI-POO). Take her—she's yours!

                                              [*Exit* KO-KO.

                        ENSEMBLE

NANKI-POO.   The threatened cloud has passed away,
YUM-YUM.   And brightly shines the dawning day;
NANKI-POO.   What though the night may come too soon,
YUM-YUM.   There's yet a month of afternoon!

           NANKI-POO, POOH-BAH, YUM-YUM, PITTI-SING,
                        and PEEP-BO

                   Then let the throng
                     Our joy advance,
                   With laughing song
                     And merry dance,

CHORUS.   With joyous shout and ringing cheer,
                   Inaugurate our brief career!

PITTI-SING.   A day, a week, a month, a year——
YUM.   Or far or near, or far or near,
POOH.   Life's eventime comes much too soon,
PITTI-SING.   You'll live at least a honeymoon!

ALL.   Then let the throng, etc.

CHORUS.   With joyous shout, etc.

SOLO—POOH-BAH

As in a month you've got to die,
    If Ko-Ko tells us true,
'Twere empty compliment to cry
    "Long life to Nanki-Poo!"
But as one month you have to live
    As fellow-citizen,
This toast with three times three we'll give—
    "Long life to you—till then!"

[Exit POOH-BAH.

CHORUS.   May all good fortune prosper you,
                    May you have health and riches too,
                    May you succeed in all you do!
                       Long life to you—till then!

(*Dance*.)

Enter KATISHA *melodramatically*

KAT.   Your revels cease! Assist me, all of you!
CHORUS.   Why, who is this whose evil eyes
                     Rain blight on our festivities?
KAT.   I claim my perjured lover, Nanki-Poo!
                  Oh, fool! to shun delights that never cloy!
CHORUS.   Go, leave thy deadly work undone!
KAT.   Come back, oh, shallow fool! come back to joy!
CHORUS.   Away, away! ill-favoured one!

NANK. (*aside to* YUM-YUM). Ah!
             'Tis Katisha!
             The maid of whom I told you. (*About to go*.)

KAT. (*detaining him*). No!
             You shall not go,
             These arms shall thus enfold you!

SONG—KATISHA

KAT. (*addressing* NANKI-POO).

> Oh fool, that fleest
> My hallowed joys!
> Oh blind, that seest
> No equipoise!
> Oh rash, that judgest
> From half, the whole!
> Oh base, that grudgest
> Love's lightest dole!
> > Thy heart unbind,
> > Oh fool, oh blind!
> > Give me my place,
> > Oh rash, oh base!

CHORUS.

> If she's thy bride, restore her place,
> Oh fool, oh blind, oh rash, oh base!

KAT. (*addressing* YUM-YUM).

> Pink cheek, that rulest
> Where wisdom serves!
> Bright eye, that foolest
> Heroic nerves!
> Rose lip, that scornest
> Lore-laden years!
> Smooth tongue, that warnest
> Who rightly hears!
> > Thy doom is nigh,
> > Pink cheek, bright eye!
> > Thy knell is rung,
> > Rose lip, smooth tongue!

CHORUS.

> If true her tale, thy knell is rung,
> Pink cheek, bright eye, rose lip, smooth tongue!

PITTI-SING.

> Away, nor prosecute your quest—
> From our intention, well expressed,
> You cannot turn us!
> The state of your connubial views

              Towards the person you accuse
                   Does not concern us!
              For he's going to marry Yum-Yum—

ALL.   Yum-Yum!

PITTI.   Your anger pray bury,
                   For all will be merry,
              I think you had better succumb—

ALL.   Cumb—cumb!

PITTI.   And join our expressions of glee.
             On this subject I pray you be dumb—

ALL.   Dumb—dumb.

PITTI.   You'll find there are many
                 Who'll wed for a penny—
            The word for your guidance is "Mum"—

ALL.   Mum—mum!

PITTI.   There's lots of good fish in the sea!

ALL.   On this subject we pray you be dumb, etc.

                SOLO—KATISHA

              The hour of gladness
                 Is dead and gone;
              In silent sadness
                 I live alone!
               The hope I cherished
                 All lifeless lies,
             And all has perished
               Save love, which never dies!
       Oh, faithless one, this insult you shall rue!
       In vain for mercy on your knees you'll sue.
         I'll tear the mask from your disguising!

NANK. (*aside*).   Now comes the blow!

KAT.   Prepare yourselves for news surprising!

NANK. (*aside*).   How foil my foe?

KAT.   No minstrel he, despite bravado!

YUM. (*aside, struck by an idea*). Ha! ha! I know!

KAT.   He is the son of your———

[NANKI-POO, YUM-YUM, *and* CHORUS, *interrupting,
sing Japanese words, to drown her voice*.

	O ni! bikkuri shakkuri to!
KAT.	In vain you interrupt with this tornado!
	He is the only son of your——
ALL.	O ni! bikkuri shakkuri to!
KAT.	I'll spoil——
ALL.	O ni! bikkuri shakkuri to!
KAT.	Your gay gambado!
	He is the son——
ALL.	O ni! bikkuri shakkuri to!
KAT.	Of your——
ALL.	O ni! bikkuri shakkuri to!
KAT.	The son of your——
ALL.	O ni! bikkuri shakkuri to! oya! oya!

ENSEMBLE

KATISHA	THE OTHERS
Ye torrents roar!	We'll hear no more,
Ye tempests howl!	Ill-omened owl,
Your wrath outpour	To joy we soar,
With angry growl!	Despite your scowl!
Do ye your worst, my vengeance call	The echoes of our festival
Shall rise triumphant over all!	Shall rise triumphant over all!
Prepare for woe,	Away you go,
Ye haughty lords,	Collect your hordes;
At once I go	Proclaim your woe
Mikado-wards,	In dismal chords;
My wrongs with vengeance shall be crowned!	We do not heed their dismal sound,
My wrongs with vengeance shall be crowned!	For joy reigns everywhere around.

[KATISHA *rushes furiously up stage, clearing the crowd away right and left,
finishing on steps at the back of stage.*

END OF ACT I

Act II

SCENE.—KO-KO's *Garden*

YUM-YUM *discovered seated at her bridal toilet, surrounded by maidens, who are dressing her hair and painting her face and lips, as she judges of the effect in a mirror.*

SOLO—PITTI-SING *and* CHORUS OF GIRLS

CHORUS.
    Braid the raven hair—
      Weave the supple tress—
    Deck the maiden fair
      In her loveliness—
    Paint the pretty face—
      Dye the coral lip—
    Emphasize the grace
      Of her ladyship!
    Art and nature, thus allied,
    Go to make a pretty bride.

SOLO—PITTI-SING

Sit with downcast eye—
  Let it brim with dew—
Try if you can cry—
  We will do so, too.
When you're summoned, start
  Like a frightened roe—
Flutter, little heart,
  Colour, come and go!
Modesty at marriage-tide
Well becomes a pretty bride!

CHORUS

Braid the raven hair, etc.

[*Exeunt* PITTI-SING, PEEP-BO, *and* CHORUS.

YUM. Yes, I am indeed beautiful! Sometimes I sit and wonder, in my artless Japanese way, why it is that I am so much more attractive than anybody else in the whole world. Can this be vanity? No! Nature is lovely and rejoices in her loveliness. I am a child of Nature, and take after my mother.

SONG—YUM-YUM

The sun, whose rays
Are all ablaze
   With ever-living glory,
Does not deny
His majesty—
   He scorns to tell a story!
He don't exclaim,
"I blush for shame,
   So kindly be indulgent."
But, fierce and bold,
In fiery gold,
   He glories all effulgent!

     I mean to rule the earth,
       As he the sky—
     We really know our worth,
       The sun and I!

Observe his flame,
That placid dame,
   The moon's Celestial Highness;
There's not a trace
Upon her face
   Of diffidence or shyness:
She borrows light
That, through the night,
   Mankind may all acclaim her!
And, truth to tell,
She lights up well,
   So I, for one, don't blame her!

     Ah, pray make no mistake,
       We are not shy;
     We're very wide awake,
       The moon and I!

Enter PITTI-SING *and* PEEP-BO

YUM. Yes, everything seems to smile upon me. I am to be married to-day to the man I love best, and I believe I am the very happiest girl in Japan!

PEEP. The happiest girl indeed, for she is indeed to be envied who has attained happiness in all but perfection.

YUM. In "all but" perfection?

PEEP. Well, dear, it can't be denied that the fact that your husband is to be beheaded in a month is, in its way, a drawback. It does seem to take the top off it, you know.

PITTI. I don't know about that. It all depends!

PEEP. At all events, *he* will find it a drawback.

PITTI. Not necessarily. Bless you, it all depends!

YUM. (*in tears*). I think it very indelicate of you to refer to such a subject on such a day. If my married happiness *is* to be—to be——

PEEP. Cut short.

YUM. Well, cut short—in a month, can't you let me forget it? (*Weeping.*)

Enter NANKI-POO, *followed by* PISH-TUSH

NANK. Yum-Yum in tears—and on her wedding morn!

YUM. (*sobbing*). They've been reminding me that in a month you're to be beheaded! (*Bursts into tears.*)

PITTI. Yes, we've been reminding her that you're to be beheaded! (*Bursts into tears.*)

PEEP. It's quite true, you know, you *are* to be beheaded! (*Bursts into tears.*)

NANK. (*aside*). Humph! Now, some bridegrooms would be depressed by this sort of thing! (*Aloud.*) A month? Well, what's a month? Bah! These divisions of time are purely arbitrary. Who says twenty-four hours make a day?

PITTI. There's a popular impression to that effect.

NANK. Then we'll efface it. We'll call each second a minute—each minute an hour—each hour a day—and each day a year. At that rate we've about thirty years of married happiness before us!

PEEP. And, at that rate, this interview has already lasted four hours and three-quarters!

[*Exit* PEEP-BO.

YUM. (*still sobbing*). Yes. How time flies when one is thoroughly enjoying oneself.

NANK. That's the way to look at it! Don't let's be downhearted! There's a silver lining to every cloud.

YUM. Certainly. Let's—let's be perfectly happy! (*Almost in tears.*)

PISH-TUSH. By all means. Let's—let's thoroughly enjoy ourselves.

PITTI. It's—it's absurd to cry. (*Trying to force a laugh.*)

YUM. Quite ridiculous! (*Trying to laugh.*)

[*All break into a forced and melancholy laugh.*

MADRIGAL

YUM-YUM, PITTI-SING, NANKI-POO, *and* PISH-TUSH

Brightly dawns our wedding day;
   Joyous hour, we give thee greeting!
   Whither, whither art thou fleeting?
Fickle moment, prithee stay!
   What though mortal joys be hollow?
   Pleasures come, if sorrows follow:
Though the tocsin sound, ere long,
   Ding dong! Ding dong!
Yet until the shadows fall
Over one and over all,
Sing a merry madrigal—
      A madrigal!

Fal-la—fal-la! etc. (*Ending in tears.*)

Let us dry the ready tear,
   Though the hours are surely creeping
   Little need for woeful weeping,
Till the sad sundown is near.
   All must sip the cup of sorrow—
   I to-day and thou to-morrow;
This the close of every song—
   Ding dong! Ding dong!
What, though solemn shadows fall,
Sooner, later, over all?
Sing a merry madrigal—
        A madrigal!

Fal-la—fal-la! etc. (*Ending in tears.*)
        [*Exeunt* PITTI-SING *and* PISH-TUSH.

[NANKI-POO *embraces* YUM-YUM. *Enter* KO-KO. NANKI-POO
        releases YUM-YUM.

KO. Go on—don't mind me.

NANK. I'm afraid we're distressing you.

KO. Never mind, I must get used to it. Only please do it by degrees.
Begin by putting your arm round her waist. (NANKI-POO *does so.*)
There; let me get used to that first.

YUM. Oh, wouldn't you like to retire? It must pain you to see us so
affectionate together!

KO. No, I must learn to bear it! Now oblige me by allowing her head
to rest on your shoulder.

NANK. Like that? (*He does so.* KO-KO *much affected.*)

KO. I am much obliged to you. Now—kiss her! (*He does so.* KO-KO
writhes with anguish.) Thank you—it's simple torture!

YUM. Come, come, bear up. After all, it's only for a month.

KO. No. It's no use deluding oneself with false hopes.

NANK.   }
          What do you mean?
YUM.   }

KO. (*to* YUM-YUM). My child—my poor child! (*Aside.*) How shall I
break it to her? (*Aloud.*) My little bride that was to have been?

YUM. (*delighted*). *Was* to have been?

KO. Yes, you never can be mine!

NANK. ⎫ (*in ecstasy*.) ⎧ What!
YUM. ⎭ ⎩ I'm so glad!

KO. I've just ascertained that, by the Mikado's law, when a married man is beheaded his wife is buried alive.

NANK. ⎫ Buried alive!
YUM. ⎭

KO. Buried alive. It's a most unpleasant death.

NANK. But whom did you get that from?

KO. Oh, from Pooh-Bah. He's my Solicitor.

YUM. But he may be mistaken!

KO. So I thought; so I consulted the Attorney-General, the Lord Chief Justice, the Master of the Rolls, the Judge Ordinary, and the Lord Chancellor. They're all of the same opinion. Never knew such unanimity on a point of law in my life!

NANK. But stop a bit! This law has never been put in force.

KO. Not yet. You see, flirting is the only crime punishable with decapitation, and married men never flirt.

NANK. Of course, they don't. I quite forgot that! Well, I suppose I may take it that my dream of happiness is at an end!

YUM. Darling—I don't want to appear selfish, and I love you with all my heart—I don't suppose I shall ever love anybody else half as much—but when I agreed to marry you—my own—I had no idea—pet—that I should have to be buried alive in a month!

NANK. Nor I! It's the very first I've heard of it!

YUM. It—it makes a difference, doesn't it?

NANK. It *does* make a difference, of course.

YUM. You see—burial alive—it's such a stuffy death!

NANK. I call it a beast of a death.

YUM. You see my difficulty, don't you?

NANK. Yes, and I see my own. If I insist on your carrying out your promise, I doom you to a hideous death: if I release you, you marry Ko-Ko at once!

TRIO—YUM-YUM, NANKI-POO, *and* KO-KO

YUM.
Here's a how-de-do!
If I marry you,
When your time has come to perish,
Then the maiden whom you cherish
Must be slaughtered, too!
Here's a how-de-do!

NANK.
Here's a pretty mess!
In a month, or less,
I must die without a wedding!
Let the bitter tears I'm shedding
Witness my distress,
Here's a pretty mess!

KO.
Here's a state of things!
To her life she clings!
Matrimonial devotion
Doesn't seem to suit her notion—
Burial it brings!
Here's a state of things!

ENSEMBLE

YUM-YUM *and* NANKI-POO	KO-KO
With a passion that's intense	With a passion that's intense
I worship and adore,	You worship and adore,
But the laws of common sense	But the laws of common sense
We oughtn't to ignore.	You oughtn't to ignore.
If what he says is true,	If what I say is true,
'Tis death to marry you!	'Tis death to marry you!
Here's a pretty state of things!	Here's a pretty state of things!
Here's a pretty how-de-do!	Here's a pretty how-de-do!

[*Exeunt* YUM-YUM.

KO. (*going up to* NANKI-POO). My poor boy, I'm really very sorry for you.

NANK. Thanks, old fellow. I'm sure you are.

KO. You see I'm quite helpless.

NANK. I quite see that.

KO. I can't conceive anything more distressing than to have one's marriage broken off at the last moment. But you shan't be disappointed of a wedding—you shall come to mine.

NANK. It's awfully kind of you, but that's impossible.

KO. Why so?

NANK. To-day I die.

KO. What do you mean?

NANK. I can't live without Yum-Yum. This afternoon I perform the Happy Despatch.

KO. No, no—pardon me—I can't allow that.

NANK. Why not?

KO. Why, hang it all, you're under contract to die by the hand of the Public Executioner in a month's time! If you kill yourself, what's to become of me? Why, I shall have to be executed in your place!

NANK. It would certainly seem so!

Enter POOH-BAH

KO. Now then, Lord Mayor, what is it?

POOH. The Mikado and his suite are approaching the city, and will be here in ten minutes.

KO. The Mikado! He's coming to see whether his orders have been carried out! (*To* NANKI-POO.) Now look here, you know—this is getting serious—a bargain's a bargain, and you really mustn't frustrate the ends of justice by committing suicide. As a man of honour and a gentleman, you are bound to die ignominiously by the hands of the Public Executioner.

NANK. Very well, then—behead me.

KO. What, now?

NANK. Certainly; at once.

POOH. Chop it off! Chop it off!

KO. My good sir, I don't go about prepared to execute gentlemen at a moment's notice. Why, I never even killed a blue-bottle!

POOH. Still, as Lord High Executioner——

KO. My good sir, as Lord High Executioner, I've got to behead him in a month. I'm not ready yet. I don't know how it's done. I'm going to take lessons. I mean to begin with a guinea pig, and work my way through the animal kingdom till I come to a Second Trombone. Why, you don't suppose that, as a humane man, I'd have accepted the post of Lord High

Executioner if I hadn't thought the duties were purely nominal? I *can't* kill you—I can't kill anything! I can't kill anybody! (*Weeps.*)

NANK. Come, my poor fellow, we all have unpleasant duties to discharge at times; after all, what is it? If I don't mind, why should you? Remember, sooner or later it must be done.

KO. (*springing up suddenly.*) *Must it?* I'm not so sure about that!

NANK. What do you mean?

KO. Why should I kill you when making an affidavit that you've been executed will do just as well? Here are plenty of witnesses—the Lord Chief Justice, Lord High Admiral, Commander-in-Chief, Secretary of State for the Home Department, First Lord of the Treasury, and Chief Commissioner of Police.

NANK. But where are they?

KO. There they are. They'll all swear to it—won't you? (*To* POOH-BAH.)

POOH. Am I to understand that all of us high Officers of State are required to perjure ourselves to ensure your safety?

KO. Why not? You'll be grossly insulted, as usual.

POOH. Will the insult be cash down, or at a date?

KO. It will be a ready-money transaction.

POOH. (*Aside.*) Well, it will be a useful discipline. (*Aloud.*) Very good. Choose your fiction, and I'll endorse it! (*Aside.*) Ha! ha! Family Pride, how do you like *that*, my buck?

NANK. But I tell you that life without Yum-Yum——

KO. Oh, Yum-Yum, Yum-Yum! Bother Yum-Yum! Here, Commissionaire (*to* POOH-BAH), go and fetch Yum-Yum. (*Exit* POOH-BAH.) Take Yum-Yum and marry Yum-Yum, only go away and never come back again. (*Enter* POOH-BAH *with* YUM-YUM.) Here she is. Yum-Yum, are you particularly busy?

YUM. Not particularly.

KO. You've five minutes to spare?

YUM. Yes.

KO. Then go along with his Grace the Archbishop of Titipu; he'll marry you at once.

YUM. But if I'm to be buried alive?

KO. Now, don't ask any questions, but do as I tell you, and Nanki-Poo will explain all.

NANK. But one moment——

KO. Not for worlds. Here comes the Mikado, no doubt to ascertain whether I've obeyed his decree, and if he finds you alive I shall have the greatest difficulty in persuading him that I've beheaded you. (*Exeunt* NANKI-POO *and* YUM-YUM, *followed by* POOH-BAH.) Close thing that, for here he comes!

[*Exit* KO-KO

March.—*Enter procession, heralding* MIKADO, *with* KATISHA
   Entrance of MIKADO *and* KATISHA
   (*"March of the Mikado's troops."*)

CHORUS.   Miya sama, miya sama,
     On n'm-ma no mayé ni
     Pira-Pira suru no wa
     Nan gia na
     Toko tonyaré tonyaré na?

DUET—MIKADO *and* KATISHA

MIK.   From every kind of man
     Obedience I expect;
   I'm the Emperor of Japan——

KAT.   And I'm his daughter-in-law elect!
     He'll marry his son
     (He's only got one)
    To his daughter-in-law elect.

MIK.   My morals have been declared
     Particularly correct;

KAT.   But they're nothing at all, compared
     With those of his daughter-in-law elect!
      Bow—Bow—
    To his daughter-in-law elect!

ALL.   Bow—Bow—
    To his daughter-in-law elect.

MIK.   In a fatherly kind of way

I govern each tribe and sect,
All cheerfully own my sway——

KAT.   Except his daughter-in-law elect!
          As tough as a bone,
          With a will of her own,
        Is his daughter-in-law elect!

MIK.   My nature is love and light—
          My freedom from all defect——

KAT.   Is insignificant quite,
          Compared with his daughter-in-law elect!
            Bow—Bow—
          To his daughter-in-law elect!

ALL.   Bow—Bow—
          To his daughter-in-law elect!

SONG—MIKADO *and* CHORUS

A more humane Mikado never
  Did in Japan exist,
    To nobody second,
    I'm certainly reckoned
  A true philanthropist.
It is my very humane endeavour

To make, to some extent,
　　Each evil liver
　　A running river
Of harmless merriment.

　　　My object all sublime
　　　I shall achieve in time—
　　To let the punishment fit the crime—
　　　　The punishment fit the crime;
　　　And make each prisoner pent
　　　Unwillingly represent
　　　A source of innocent merriment!
　　　　Of innocent merriment!

All prosy dull society sinners,
　　Who chatter and bleat and bore,
　　　Are sent to hear sermons
　　　From mystical Germans
　　Who preach from ten till four.
The amateur tenor, whose vocal villainies
　　All desire to shirk,
　　　Shall, during off-hours,
　　　Exhibit his powers
　　To Madame Tussaud's waxwork.

The lady who dyes a chemical yellow
　　Or stains her grey hair puce,
　　　Or pinches her figger,
　　　Is painted with vigour[1]
　　With permanent walnut juice.
The idiot who, in railway carriages,
　　Scribbles on window-panes,
　　　We only suffer
　　　To ride on a buffer
　　In Parliamentary trains.

　　　My object all sublime, etc.

---

[1] The original line, "Is blacked like a nigger" (referring to blackface performers), has been thus replaced in modern performances.

CHORUS.   His object all sublime, etc.

> The advertising quack who wearies
>   With tales of countless cures,
>   His teeth, I've enacted,
>   Shall all be extracted
>   By terrified amateurs.
> The music-hall singer attends a series
>   Of masses and fugues and "ops"
>   By Bach, interwoven
>   With Spohr and Beethoven,
>   At classical Monday Pops.

> The billiard sharp whom any one catches,
>   His doom's extremely hard—
>   He's made to dwell—
>   In a dungeon cell
>   On a spot that's always barred.
> And there he plays extravagant matches
>   In fitless finger-stalls
>   On a cloth untrue,
>   With a twisted cue
>   And elliptical billiard balls!

                  My object all sublime, etc.

CHORUS.   His object all sublime, etc.

Enter POOH-BAH, KO-KO, *and* PITTI-SING. *All kneel.*

(POOH-BAH *hands a paper to* KO-KO.)

KO. I am honoured in being permitted to welcome your Majesty. I guess the object of your Majesty's visit—your wishes have been attended to. The execution has taken place.

MIK. Oh, you've had an execution, have you?

KO. Yes. The Coroner has just handed me his certificate.

POOH. I am the Coroner. (KO-KO *hands certificate to* MIKADO.)

MIK. And this is the certificate of his death. (*Reads.*) "At Titipu, in the presence of the Lord Chancellor, Lord Chief Justice, Attorney-General, Secretary of State for the Home Department, Lord Mayor, and Groom of the Second Floor Front——"

POOH. They were all present, your Majesty. I counted them myself.

MIK. Very good house. I wish I'd been in time for the performance.

KO. A tough fellow he was, too—a man of gigantic strength. His struggles were terrific. It was really a remarkable scene.

MIK. Describe it.

TRIO AND CHORUS

KO-KO, PITTI-SING, POOH-BAH *and* CHORUS

KO.
The criminal cried, as he dropped him down,
 In a state of wild alarm—
With a frightful, frantic, fearful frown,
 I bared my big right arm.
I seized him by his little pig-tail,
 And on his knees fell he,
  As he squirmed and struggled,
  And gurgled and guggled,
 I drew my snickersnee!
  Oh, never shall I
  Forget the cry,
Or the shriek that shriekèd he,
  As I gnashed my teeth,
  When from its sheath
 I drew my snickersnee!

CHORUS

 We know him well,
 He cannot tell
Untrue or groundless tales—
 He always tries
 To utter lies,
And every time he fails.

PITTI.
He shivered and shook as he gave the sign
 For the stroke he didn't deserve;
When all of a sudden his eye met mine,
 And it seemed to brace his nerve;
For he nodded his head and kissed his hand,

And he whistled an air, did he,
　　As the sabre true
　　Cut cleanly through
His cervical vertebræ!
　　When a man's afraid,
　　A beautiful maid
Is a cheering sight to see;
　　And it's oh, I'm glad
　　That moment sad
Was soothed by sight of me!

CHORUS

　　Her terrible tale
　　You can't assail,
With truth it quite agrees:
　　Her taste exact
　　For faultless fact
Amounts to a disease.

POOH.　　Now though you'd have said that head was dead
　　　(For its owner dead was he),
It stood on its neck, with a smile well-bred,
　　And bowed three times to me!
It was none of your impudent off-hand nods,
　　But as humble as could be;
　　　For it clearly knew
　　　The deference due
To a man of pedigree!
　　　And it's oh, I vow,
　　　This deathly bow
Was a touching sight to see;
　　　Though trunkless, yet
　　　It couldn't forget
The deference due to me!

CHORUS

This haughty youth,
He speaks the truth
Whenever he finds it pays:
And in this case
It all took place
Exactly as he says!

[*Exeunt* CHORUS.

MIK. All this is very interesting, and I should like to have seen it. But we came about a totally different matter. A year ago my son, the heir to the throne of Japan, bolted from our Imperial Court.

KO. Indeed! Had he any reason to be dissatisfied with his position?

KAT. None whatever. On the contrary, I was going to marry him—yet he fled!

POOH. I am surprised that he should have fled from one so lovely!

KAT. That's not true.

POOH. No!

KAT. You hold that I am not beautiful because my face is plain. But you know nothing; you are still unenlightened. Learn, then, that it is not in the face alone that beauty is to be sought. My face is unattractive!

POOH. It is.

KAT. But I have a left shoulder-blade that is a miracle of loveliness. People come miles to see it. My right elbow has a fascination that few can resist.

POOH. Allow me!

KAT. It is on view Tuesdays and Fridays, on presentation of visiting card. As for my circulation, it is the largest in the world.

KO. And yet he fled!

MIK. And is now masquerading in this town, disguised as a Second Trombone.

KO.
POOH. } A Second Trombone!
PITTI.

MIK. Yes; would it be troubling you too much if I asked you to produce him? He goes by the name of——

KAT. Nanki-Poo.

MIK. Nanki-Poo.

KO. It's quite easy. That is, it's rather difficult. In point of fact, he's gone abroad!

MIK. Gone abroad! His address.

KO. Knightsbridge!

KAT. (*who is reading certificate of death*). Ha!

MIK. What's the matter?

KAT. See here—his name—Nanki-Poo—beheaded this morning. Oh, where shall I find another? Where shall I find another?

[KO-KO, POOH-BAH, *and* PITTI-SING *fall on their knees.*

MIK. (*looking at paper*). Dear, dear, dear! this is very tiresome. (*To* KO-KO.) My poor fellow, in your anxiety to carry out my wishes you have beheaded the heir to the throne of Japan!

KO. I beg to offer an unqualified apology.

POOH. I desire to associate myself with that expression of regret.

PITTI. We really hadn't the least notion——

MIK. Of course you hadn't. How could you? Come, come, my good fellow, don't distress yourself—it was no fault of yours. If a man of exalted rank chooses to disguise himself as a Second Trombone, he must take the consequences. It really distresses me to see you take on so. I've no doubt he thoroughly deserved all he got. (*They rise.*)

KO. We are infinitely obliged to your Majesty——

PITTI. Much obliged, your Majesty.

POOH. Very much obliged, your Majesty.

MIK. Obliged? not a bit. Don't mention it. How *could* you tell?

POOH. No, of course we couldn't tell who the gentleman really was.

PITTI. It wasn't written on his forehead, you know.

KO. It might have been on his pocket-handkerchief, but Japanese don't use pocket-handkerchiefs! Ha! ha! ha!

MIK. Ha! ha! ha! (*To* KATISHA.) I forget the punishment for compassing the death of the Heir Apparent.

KO. ⎫
POOH. ⎬ Punishment. (*They drop down on their knees again.*)
PITTI. ⎭

MIK. Yes. Something lingering, with boiling oil in it, I fancy. Something of that sort. I think boiling oil occurs in it, but I'm not sure. I know it's something humorous, but lingering, with either boiling oil or melted lead. Come, come, don't fret—I'm not a bit angry.

KO. (*in abject terror*). If your Majesty will accept our assurance, we had no idea——

MIK. Of course——

PITTI. I knew nothing about it.

POOH. I wasn't there.

MIK. That's the pathetic part of it. Unfortunately, the fool of an Act says "compassing the death of the Heir Apparent." There's not a word about a mistake——

KO., PITTI., *and* POOH. No!

MIK. Or not knowing——

KO. No!

MIK. Or having no notion——

PITTI. No!

MIK. Or not being there——

POOH. No!

MIK. There should be, of course——

KO., PITTI., *and* POOH. Yes!

MIK. But there isn't.

KO., PITTI., *and* POOH. Oh!

MIK. That's the slovenly way in which these Acts are always drawn. However, cheer up, it'll be all right. I'll have it altered next session. Now, let's see about your execution—will after luncheon suit you? Can you wait till then?

KO., PITTI., *and* POOH. Oh, yes—we can wait till then!

MIK. Then we'll make it after luncheon.

POOH. I don't want any lunch.

MIK. I'm really very sorry for you all, but it's an unjust world, and virtue is triumphant only in theatrical performances.

GLEE

PITTI-SING, KATISHA, KO-KO, POOH-BAH, *and* MIKADO

MIK.   See how the Fates their gifts allot,
            For A is happy—B is not.
            Yet B is worthy, I dare say,
            Of more prosperity than A!

KO., POOH., *and* PITTI. *Is* B more worthy?

KAT.   I should say
He's worth a great deal more than A.

ENSEMBLE
> Yet A is happy!
>   Oh, so happy!
> Laughing, Ha! ha!
> Chaffing, Ha! ha!
> Nectar quaffing, Ha! ha! ha!
> Ever joyous, ever gay,
> Happy, undeserving A!

KO., POOH., *and* PITTI.

> If I were Fortune—which I'm not—
> B should enjoy A's happy lot,
> And A should die in miserie—
> That is, assuming I am B.

MIK. *and* KAT.   But *should* A perish?

KO., POOH., *and* PITTI.   That should he
> (Of course, assuming I am B).
> B should be happy!
>   Oh, so happy!
> Laughing, Ha! ha!
> Chafing, Ha! ha!
> Nectar quaffing, Ha! ha! ha!
> But condemned to die is he,
> Wretched meritorious B!

[*Exeunt* MIKADO *and* KATISHA.

KO. Well, a nice mess you've got us into, with your nodding head and the deference due to a man of pedigree!

POOH. Merely corroborative detail, intended to give artistic verisimilitude to an otherwise bald and unconvincing narrative.

PITTI. Corroborative detail indeed! Corroborative fiddlestick!

KO. And you're just as bad as he is with your cock-and-a-bull stories about catching his eye and his whistling an air. But that's so like you! You must put in your oar!

POOH. But how about your big right arm?

PITTI. Yes, and your snickersnee!

KO. Well, well, never mind that now. There's only one thing to be done. Nanki-Poo hasn't started yet—he must come to life again at once. (*Enter* NANKI-POO *and* YUM-YUM *prepared for journey.*) Here he comes. Here, Nanki-Poo, I've good news for you—you're reprieved.

NANK. Oh, but it's too late. I'm a dead man, and I'm off for my honeymoon.

KO. Nonsense! A terrible thing has just happened. It seems you're the son of the Mikado.

NANK. Yes, but that happened some time ago.

KO. Is this a time for airy persiflage? Your father is here, and with Katisha!

NANK. My father! And with Katisha!

KO. Yes, he wants you particularly.

POOH. So does she.

YUM. Oh, but he's married now.

KO. But, bless my heart! what has that to do with it?

NANK. Katisha claims me in marriage, but I can't marry her because I'm married already—consequently she will insist on my execution, and if I'm executed, my wife will have to be buried alive.

YUM. You see our difficulty.

KO. Yes. I don't know what's to be done.

NANK. There's one chance for you. If you could persuade Katisha to marry you, she would have no further claim on me, and in that case I could come to life without any fear of being put to death.

KO. I marry Katisha!

YUM. I really think it's the only course.

KO. But, my good girl, have you seen her? She's something appalling!

PITTI. Ah! that's only her face. She has a left elbow which people come miles to see!

POOH. I am told that her right heel is much admired by connoisseurs.

KO. My good sir, I decline to pin my heart upon any lady's right heel.

NANK. It comes to this: While Katisha is single, I prefer to be a disembodied spirit. When Katisha is married, existence will be as welcome as the flowers in spring.

DUET—NANKI-POO *and* KO-KO

(*With* YUM-YUM, PITTI-SING, *and* POOH-BAH)

NANK.   The flowers that bloom in the spring,
             Tra la,
      Breathe promise of merry sunshine—
    As we merrily dance and we sing,
             Tra la,
    We welcome the hope that they bring,
             Tra la,
      Of a summer of roses and wine.
        And that's what we mean when we say that a thing
        Is welcome as flowers that bloom in the spring.
            Tra la la la la la, etc.

ALL.   Tra la la la la, etc.

KO.   The flowers that bloom in the spring,
             Tra la,
      Have nothing to do with the case.
    I've got to take under my wing,
             Tra la,
    A most unattractive old thing,
             Tra la,
      With a caricature of a face,
      And that's what I mean when I say, or I sing,
      "Oh, bother the flowers that bloom in the spring."
            Tra la la la la la, etc.

ALL.   Tra la la la, Tra la la la, etc.
       [*Dance and exeunt* NANKI-POO, YUM-YUM,
         POOH-BAH, PITTI-SING, *and* KO-KO.

Enter KATISHA

RECITATIVE *and* SONG—KATISHA

Alone, and yet alive! Oh, sepulchre!
My soul is still my body's prisoner!

Remote the peace that Death alone can give—
My doom, to wait! my punishment, to live!

SONG

Hearts do not break!
They sting and ache
For old love's sake,
    But do not die,
Though with each breath
They long for death
As witnesseth
    The living I!
        Oh, living I!
        Come, tell me why,
        When hope is gone,
        Dost thou stay on?
        Why linger here,
        Where all is drear?
        Oh, living I!
        Come, tell me why,
        When hope is gone,
        Dost thou stay on?
    May not a cheated maiden die?

KO. (*entering and approaching her timidly*). Katisha!

KAT. The miscreant who robbed me of my love! But vengeance pursues—they are heating the cauldron!

KO. Katisha—behold a suppliant at your feet! Katisha—mercy!

KAT. Mercy? Had you mercy on him? See him, you! You have slain my love. He did not love *me*, but he would have loved me in time. I am an acquired taste—only the educated palate can appreciate *me*. I was educating *his* palate when he left me. Well, he is dead, and where shall I find another? It takes years to train a man to love me. Am I to go through the weary round again, and, at the same time, implore mercy for you who robbed me of my prey—I mean my pupil—just as his education was on the point of completion? Oh, where shall I find another?

KO. (*suddenly, and with great vehemence*). Here!—Here!

KAT. What!!!

KO. (*with intense passion*). Katisha, for years I have loved you with a white-hot passion that is slowly but surely consuming my very vitals! Ah, shrink not from me! If there is aught of woman's mercy in your heart, turn not away from a love-sick suppliant whose every fibre thrills at your tiniest touch! True it is that, under a poor mask of disgust, I have endeavoured to conceal a passion whose inner fires are broiling the soul within me! But the fire will not be smothered—it defies all attempts at extinction, and, breaking forth, all the more eagerly for its long restraint, it declares itself in words that will not be weighed—that cannot be schooled—that should not be too severely criticised. Katisha, I dare not hope for your love—but I will not live without it! Darling!

KAT. You, whose hands still reek with the blood of my betrothed, dare to address words of passion to the woman you have so foully wronged!

KO. I do—accept my love, or I perish on the spot!

KAT. Go to! Who knows so well as I that no one ever yet died of a broken heart!

KO. You know not what you say. Listen!

SONG—KO-KO

On a tree by a river a little tom-tit
     Sang "Willow, titwillow, titwillow!"
And I said to him, "Dicky-bird, why do you sit
     Singing 'Willow, titwillow, titwillow'?"
"Is it weakness of intellect, birdie?" I cried,
"Or a rather tough worm in your little inside?"
With a shake of his poor little head, he replied,
     "Oh, willow, titwillow, titwillow!"

He slapped at his chest, as he sat on that bough,
     Singing "Willow, titwillow, titwillow!"
And a cold perspiration bespangled his brow,
     Oh, willow, titwillow, titwillow!
He sobbed and he sighed, and a gurgle he gave,
Then he plunged himself into the billowy wave,
And an echo arose from the suicide's grave—
     "Oh, willow, titwillow, titwillow!"

Now I feel just as sure as I'm sure that my name
     Isn't Willow, titwillow, titwillow,
That 'twas blighted affection that made him exclaim
     "Oh, willow, titwillow, titwillow!"
And if you remain callous and obdurate, I
Shall perish as he did, and you will know why,
Though I probably shall not exclaim as I die,
     "Oh, willow, titwillow, titwillow!"

[*During this song* KATISHA *has been greatly
affected, and at the end is almost in tears.*

KAT. (*whimpering*). Did he really die of love?

KO. He really did.

KAT. All on account of a cruel little hen?

KO. Yes.

KAT. Poor little chap!

KO. It's an affecting tale, and quite true. I knew the bird intimately.

KAT. Did you? He must have been very fond of her.

KO. His devotion was something extraordinary.

KAT. (*still whimpering*). Poor little chap! And—and if I refuse you, will you go and do the same?

KO. At once.

KAT. No, no—you mustn't! Anything but that! (*Falls on his breast.*) Oh, I'm a silly little goose!

KO. (*making a wry face*). You are!

KAT. And you won't hate me because I'm just a little teeny weeny wee bit bloodthirsty, will you?

KO. Hate you? Oh, Katisha! is there not beauty even in bloodthirstiness?

KAT. My idea exactly.

DUET—KATISHA *and* KO-KO

KAT.
There is beauty in the bellow of the blast,
There is grandeur in the growling of the gale,
There is eloquent outpouring
When the lion is a-roaring,
And the tiger is a-lashing of his tail!

KO.
Yes, I like to see a tiger
From the Congo or the Niger,
And especially when lashing of his tail!

KAT.
Volcanoes have a splendour that is grim,
And earthquakes only terrify the dolts,
But to him who's scientific
There's nothing that's terrific
In the falling of a flight of thunderbolts!

KO.
Yes, in spite of all my meekness,
If I have a little weakness,
It's a passion for a flight of thunderbolts!

BOTH.   If that is so,
                    Sing derry down derry!
                    It's evident, very,
                        Our tastes are one.
                Away we'll go,
                    And merrily marry,
                    Nor tardily tarry
                        Till day is done!

KO.   There is beauty in extreme old age—
                    Do you fancy you are elderly enough?
                    Information I'm requesting
                    On a subject interesting:
                    Is a maiden all the better when she's tough?
KAT.   Throughout this wide dominion
                    It's the general opinion
                That she'll last a good deal longer when she's tough.
KO.   Are you old enough to marry, do you think?
                    Won't you wait till you are eighty in the shade?
                    There's a fascination frantic
                    In a ruin that's romantic;
                    Do you think you are sufficiently decayed?
KAT.   To the matter that you mention
                    I have given some attention,
                And I think I am sufficiently decayed.

BOTH.   If that is so,
                    Sing derry down derry!
                    It's evident, very,
                        Our tastes are one!
                Away we'll go,
                    And merrily marry,
                    Nor tardily tarry
                        Till day is done!

                                        [*Exeunt together*.

Flourish. Enter the MIKADO, *attended by* PISH-TUSH *and Court*

MIK. Now then, we've had a capital lunch, and we're quite ready. Have all the painful preparations been made?

PISH. Your Majesty, all is prepared.

MIK. Then produce the unfortunate gentleman and his two well-meaning but misguided accomplices.

Enter KO-KO, KATISHA, POOH-BAH, *and* PITTI-SING. *They throw themselves at the* MIKADO's *feet*

KAT. Mercy! Mercy for Ko-Ko! Mercy for Pitti-Sing! Mercy even for Pooh-Bah!

MIK. I beg your pardon, I don't think I quite caught that remark.

POOH. Mercy even for Pooh-Bah.

KAT. Mercy! My husband that was to have been is dead, and I have just married this miserable object.

MIK. Oh! You've not been long about it!

KO. We were married before the Registrar.

POOH. *I* am the Registrar.

MIK. I see. But my difficulty is that, as you have slain the Heir Apparent——

Enter NANKI-POO *and* YUM-YUM. *They kneel*

NANKI. The Heir Apparent is *not* slain.

MIK. Bless my heart, my son!

YUM. And your daughter-in-law elected!

KAT. (*seizing* KO-KO). Traitor, you have deceived me!

MIK. Yes, you are entitled to a little explanation, but I think he will give it better whole than in pieces.

KO. Your Majesty, it's like this: It is true that I stated that I had killed Nanki-Poo——

MIK. Yes, with most affecting particulars.

POOH. Merely corroborative detail intended to give artistic verisimilitude to a bald and——

KO. *Will* you refrain from putting in your oar? (*To* MIKADO.) It's like this: When your Majesty says, "Let a thing be done," it's as good as done—practically, it *is* done—because your Majesty's will is law. Your Majesty says, "Kill a gentleman," and a gentleman is told off to be killed. Consequently, that gentleman is as good as dead—practically, he *is* dead—and if he is dead, why not say so?

MIK. I see. Nothing could possibly be more satisfactory!

FINALE

PITTI.	For he's gone and married Yum-Yum—
ALL.	Yum-Yum!
PITTI.	Your anger pray bury, For all will be merry, I think you had better succumb—
ALL.	Cumb—cumb!
PITTI.	And join our expressions of glee!
KO.	On this subject I pray you be dumb—
ALL.	Dumb—dumb!
KO.	Your notions, though many, Are not worth a penny, The word for your guidance is "Mum"—
ALL.	Mum—Mum!
KO.	You've a very good bargain in me.
ALL.	On this subject we pray you be dumb— Dumb—dumb! We think you had better succumb— Cumb—cumb! You'll find there are many Who'll wed for a penny, There are lots of good fish in the sea.
YUM. *and* NANK.	The threatened cloud has passed away, And brightly shines the dawning day; What though the night may come too soon. We've years and years of afternoon!
ALL.	Then let the throng Our joy advance, With laughing song And merry dance, With joyous shout and ringing cheer, Inaugurate our new career! Then let the throng, etc.

CURTAIN

DOVER · THRIFT · EDITIONS

FICTION

FLATLAND: A ROMANCE OF MANY DIMENSIONS, Edwin A. Abbott. 96pp. 27263-X $1.00

PERSUASION, Jane Austen. 224pp. 29555-9 $2.00

PRIDE AND PREJUDICE, Jane Austen. 272pp. 28473-5 $2.00

SENSE AND SENSIBILITY, Jane Austen. 272pp. 29049-2 $2.00

WUTHERING HEIGHTS, Emily Brontë. 256pp. 29256-8 $2.00

BEOWULF, Beowulf (trans. by R. K. Gordon). 64pp. 27264-8 $1.00

CIVIL WAR STORIES, Ambrose Bierce. 128pp. 28038-1 $1.00

THE AUTOBIOGRAPHY OF AN EX-COLORED MAN, James Weldon Johnson. 112pp. 28512-X $1.00

TARZAN OF THE APES, Edgar Rice Burroughs. 224pp. (Available in U.S. only) 29570-2 $2.00

ALICE'S ADVENTURES IN WONDERLAND, Lewis Carroll. 96pp. 27543-4 $1.00

O PIONEERS!, Willa Cather. 128pp. 27785-2 $1.00

MY ÁNTONIA, Willa Cather. 176pp. 28240-6 $2.00

PAUL'S CASE AND OTHER STORIES, Willa Cather. 64pp. 29057-3 $1.00

IN A GERMAN PENSION: 13 Stories, Katherine Mansfield. 112pp. 28719-X $1.50

THE STORY OF AN AFRICAN FARM, Olive Schreiner. 256pp. 40165-0 $2.00

"THE YELLOW WALLPAPER" AND OTHER STORIES, Charlotte Perkins Gilman. 80pp. 29857-4 $1.00

HERLAND, Charlotte Perkins Gilman. 128pp. 40429-3 $1.50

FIVE GREAT SHORT STORIES, Anton Chekhov. 96pp. 26463-7 $1.00

"THE FIDDLER OF THE REELS" AND OTHER SHORT STORIES, Thomas Hardy. 80pp. 29960-0 $1.50

FAVORITE FATHER BROWN STORIES, G. K. Chesterton. 96pp. 27545-0 $1.00

THE WARDEN, Anthony Trollope. 176pp. 40076-X $2.00

THE COUNTRY OF THE POINTED FIRS, Sarah Orne Jewett. 96pp. 28196-5 $1.00

GREAT SHORT STORIES BY AMERICAN WOMEN, Candace Ward (ed.). 192pp. 28776-9 $2.00

SHORT STORIES, Louisa May Alcott. 64pp. 29063-8 $1.00

THE AWAKENING, Kate Chopin. 128pp. 27786-0 $1.00

A PAIR OF SILK STOCKINGS AND OTHER STORIES, Kate Chopin. 64pp. 29264-9 $1.00

THE REVOLT OF "MOTHER" AND OTHER STORIES, Mary E. Wilkins Freeman. 128pp. 40428-5 $1.50

HEART OF DARKNESS, Joseph Conrad. 80pp. 26464-5 $1.00

THE SECRET SHARER AND OTHER STORIES, Joseph Conrad. 128pp. 27546-9 $1.00

THE "LITTLE REGIMENT" AND OTHER CIVIL WAR STORIES, Stephen Crane. 80pp. 29557-5 $1.00

THE OPEN BOAT AND OTHER STORIES, Stephen Crane. 128pp. 27547-7 $1.50

THE RED BADGE OF COURAGE, Stephen Crane. 112pp. 26465-3 $1.00

A CHRISTMAS CAROL, Charles Dickens. 80pp. 26865-9 $1.00

THE CRICKET ON THE HEARTH AND OTHER CHRISTMAS STORIES, Charles Dickens. 128pp. 28039-X $1.00

THE DOUBLE, Fyodor Dostoyevsky. 128pp. 29572-9 $1.50

NOTES FROM THE UNDERGROUND, Fyodor Dostoyevsky. 96pp. 27053-X $1.00

THE GAMBLER, Fyodor Dostoyevsky. 112pp. 29081-6 $1.50

THE ADVENTURE OF THE DANCING MEN AND OTHER STORIES, Sir Arthur Conan Doyle. 80pp. 29558-3 $1.00

THE HOUND OF THE BASKERVILLES, Arthur Conan Doyle. 128pp. 28214-7 $1.00

SIX GREAT SHERLOCK HOLMES STORIES, Sir Arthur Conan Doyle. 112pp. 27055-6 $1.00

SILAS MARNER, George Eliot. 160pp. 29246-0 $1.50